MW01131857

Flagstone Elementary LMC
104 Lovington St.
Castle Rock, CO 80104

LINDA BOZZO

Amazing Animal Teeth

PowerKiDS
press
New York

To my family and friends and all of your amazing features that make you who you are.
—LBS

Published in 2008 by The Rosen Publishing Group, Inc.
29 East 21st Street, New York, NY 10010

First Edition

Editor: Joanne Randolph
Book Design: Kate Laczynski
Photo Researcher: Nicole Pristash

Photo Credits: Cover © www.istockphoto.com/Hedda Gjerpen; p. 5, 13, 15, 19, 21 Shutterstock.com; p. 7 © John Cancalosi/Peter Arnold, Inc.; p. 9 © www.istockphoto.com/Nancy Nehring; p. 11, 17 © SuperStock, Inc.

Library of Congress Cataloging-in-Publication Data

Bozzo, Linda.
  Amazing animal teeth / Linda Bozzo. — 1st ed.
    p. cm. — (Creature features)
  Includes index.
  ISBN 978-1-4042-4170-1 (library binding)
  1. Teeth—Juvenile literature. I. Title.
  QL858.B69 2008
  591.4'4—dc22
                                              2007025883

Manufactured in the United States of America

CONTENTS

A LOOK INSIDE

Chomp! Tear! Bite! Chew! These are just some of the things that teeth can do. Teeth come in many shapes and sizes. Over time, animals' teeth have **adapted** to their **habitat** and the kind of food the animals eat. If an animal could not eat, it would die. That is why adapting is so important.

Not all animals use their teeth just to eat. Teeth can be used for things like fighting or scaring away other animals. Here is a look inside the mouth of a few of the animals with amazing teeth.

A hippo's teeth are used for eating grasses and plants and for keeping the hippo safe. The hippo fights with its largest teeth.

FANGS!

Snakes may not have arms and legs, but they do have teeth! A snake catches its **prey** with its teeth. A snake's teeth are pointed backward to help it catch and hold on to its food. Because of this, a snake cannot chew. It must swallow its prey whole.

Poisonous snakes have special teeth called **fangs**. Fangs are sharp, **hollow** teeth. When a snake bites its prey, **venom** comes out through the fangs. Some snakes have really long fangs. These fangs fold back into their mouth. If they did not, the snake would bite itself. Ouch!

When a snake loses or breaks a fang, a new one will grow in its place. This rattlesnake's fangs can be seen as the snake opens its mouth to strike.

RINGS AROUND THE TEETH

Some types of dolphins have more teeth than any other **mammal**. These dolphins have more than 200 teeth! Other dolphins have as few as 4 teeth. No matter how many teeth a dolphin has, the teeth are sharp and shaped liked cones. This is a perfect shape to allow dolphins to catch and hold on to their slippery, fast-moving prey.

Dolphins grow only one set of teeth during their life. Like a tree, the age of a dolphin can be told by counting the rings around its teeth.

Dolphins do not use their teeth to chew their food. They may tear their food into chunks or swallow it whole.

FAST EATERS

A school of piranhas is one kind of school you want to stay far away from! A piranha is a fish that is famous for its sharp teeth. A piranha's teeth are shaped like triangles. The top and bottom teeth work like a trap. When a piranha bites its prey, its teeth rip out large pieces of flesh.

Piranhas never chew their food. They swallow each bite whole. This is how a piranha eats its food so fast. A school of piranhas can clean all the meat off a large animal in just a few seconds.

Here you can see the piranha's sharp, triangular teeth. Piranhas live in rivers in South America.

REALLY BIG TEETH

An animal may see a flash of orange right before a tiger rushes in for the kill. With its front paws, the tiger grabs its prey and brings it to the ground. The tiger then kills the animal by biting it on the neck. This is not a happy ending for the prey, but the tiger needs to eat meat to live.

A tiger generally has 30 teeth, all made to tear and eat flesh. The tiger has the largest **canines** of all the big cats. These teeth are up to about 3 inches (8 cm) long!

Do you see the large canines that the tiger uses to kill its prey? After eating a large animal, this tiger will not have to eat again for a week!

BORN TO CHEW

Very few animals are born with teeth. A hamster's teeth can be seen from the time the hamster is born, though. This animal truly is born to chew!

A hamster's teeth never stop growing. The hamster needs to chew on something hard all the time to wear them down. If it did not wear down its teeth, they would get too long. This would be a real problem. The hamster would not be able to close its mouth or chew. If the hamster was not able to eat, it would die.

Hamsters are commonly kept as pets. They must be given something to chew to keep their teeth from growing too long.

ROWS AND ROWS OF TEETH

Everyone out of the water! There is a shark! A shark might be the first animal you think of when you think of sharp teeth. Not all sharks have the same kind of teeth, though. Some sharks have pointed teeth to hold and tear their prey. Other sharks have strong, flat teeth to **crush** crab shells. There are even sharks with curved teeth to catch fish.

Sharks can have up to 3,000 teeth in their mouth at one time. These teeth are lined up in rows. When a shark's tooth is lost or broken, a new tooth moves up to take its place.

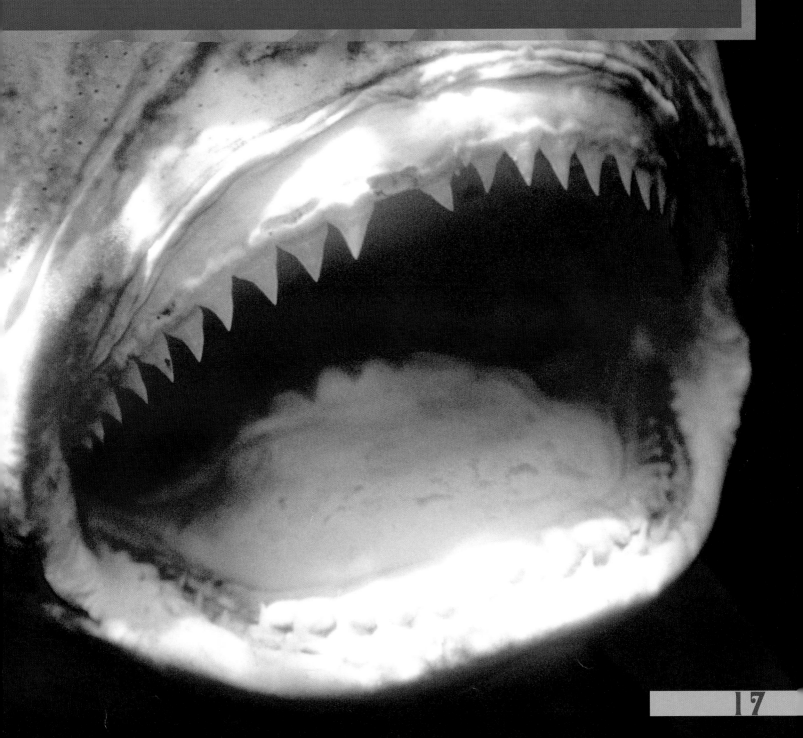

This is a great white shark's mouth. Great whites can have teeth that are up to 3 inches (8 cm) long!

TUSKS ARE TEETH

An elephant eats its food with only four teeth in its mouth! It has two teeth on the top and two on the bottom. Even though these teeth are big, they wear down. When a tooth gets worn down, it gets pushed out. A new tooth grows in from behind it.

During its life, an elephant goes through six sets of teeth. Some elephants have tusks. Tusks are two long teeth that elephants use to dig for water. They also use them to dig up the roots of trees, which they like to eat. Some elephants even fight with their tusks.

A male elephant's tusks grow up to 7 inches (18 cm) each year. Unfortunately, hunters kill many elephants to take their tusks.

A WHOLE LOT OF TEETH

Some crocodiles have more than 100 teeth. It might surprise some people that crocodiles do not chew with their teeth. A crocodile's teeth are good for holding and cutting prey. They are not good for chewing.

These animals often lose teeth in their struggle with their prey. For a crocodile, this is not a problem. Because the crocodile loses or wears out its teeth often, new teeth grow its whole life. That is a lot of new teeth since some crocodiles have lived to be over 100 years old.

This crocodile has just caught a fish in its teeth. This crocodile lives in the Nile River, in Africa.

Teeth are just one of the many amazing **features** these animals have. They are also one of the most important features. Just like you do, all animals need to eat. Over time, each animal's teeth have become specialized. This means they are made to help the animal catch and eat the foods they like best and the foods they need to live.

Teeth catch, crush, tear, and sometimes chew food. Some animals have small teeth. Some have large ones. Some animals have sharp teeth. Others have large, flat teeth. An animal's teeth are full of clues about what the animal eats. Open wide!

GLOSSARY

adapted (uh-DAPT-ed) Changed to fit requirements.

canines (KAY-nynz) Pointy teeth found on the sides of the mouth, in front.

crush (KRUSH) To destroy something by pressing.

fangs (FANGZ) Sharp teeth that inject venom.

features (FEE-churz) The special look or form of a person, an animal, or an object.

habitat (HA-beh-tat) The kind of land where an animal or a plant naturally lives.

hollow (HOL-oh) Having a hole through the center.

mammal (MA-mul) A warm-blooded animal that has a backbone and hair, breathes air, and feeds milk to its young.

poisonous (POYZ-nus) Causing pain or death.

prey (PRAY) An animal that is hunted by another animal for food.

venom (VEH-num) A poison passed by one animal into another through a bite or a sting.

INDEX

WEB SITES

Due to the changing nature of Internet links, PowerKids Press has developed an online list of Web sites related to the subject of this book. This site is updated regularly. Please use this link to access the list:

www.powerkidslinks.com/cfeat/teeth/